Employers are responsible for providing a safe and healthful workplace for their employees. OSHA's role is to assure the safety and health of America's working men and women by setting and enforcing standards; providing training, outreach and education; establishing partnerships; and encouraging continual improvement in workplace safety and health.

This handbook provides a general overview of a particular topic related to OSHA standards. It does not alter or determine compliance responsibilities in OSHA standards or the *Occupational Safety and Health Act of 1970*. Because interpretations and enforcement policy may change over time, you should consult current OSHA administrative interpretations and decisions by the Occupational Safety and Health Review Commission and the courts for additional guidance on OSHA compliance requirements.

This information is available to sensory impaired individuals upon request. Voice phone: (202) 693-1999; teletypewriter (TTY) number: (877) 889-5627.

Preparing and Protecting Security Personnel in Emergencies

U.S. Department of Labor

Occupational Safety and Health Administration

OSHA 3335-10N
2007

Contents

Introduction

Security personnel (i.e., guards) potentially risk occupational exposures to hazardous substances including chemical, biological, radiological, and nuclear (CBRN) materials during emergencies. Emergencies involving the release of hazardous chemicals at industrial facilities, including chemical manufacturers and industrial facilities utilizing hazardous substances, are the most likely and predictable incidents that may involve security personnel. Security personnel, however, work at a variety of locations with the potential for emergency incidents. Although general chemical release emergencies may be the most likely, incidents resulting from natural disasters or involving weapons of mass destruction (WMD) are also of concern to both private and public sector employers and the security personnel they employ. Security personnel working at companies for the protection of the facilities, materials, and products, as well as those employed by government agencies, are often called upon to provide support during hazardous substance emergencies and the emergency planning in preparation for such incidents is key to successful implementation of emergency response operations.

This document specifically addresses emergencies involving hazardous substance releases and provides guidance for employers, and their security personnel, who may be involved in the emergency response. It does not address other safety and health hazards (e.g., workplace violence) that security personnel may be exposed to while performing their routine duties.

The role that security personnel will have in an emergency is important with respect to the success of emergency response operations. The role they are assigned by their employer is also important in determining the training, information, and personal protective equipment they must be provided to safely perform their duties. In many cases, they will be the first individuals to a release scene and their role in such cases must be clearly understood. Security personnel who are expected by their employer to provide support during an emergency involving a hazardous substance

release, arising from natural disasters, or involving WMDs must receive training in accordance with OSHA requirements. Security personnel expected by their employer to assume an emergency responder role during a hazardous substance release are covered by OSHA's Hazardous Waste Operations and Emergency Response (HAZWOPER) standard, or the parallel OSHA-approved State Plan standards. OSHA's HAZWOPER standard, 29 CFR 1910.120, describes the level of training for personnel involved in emergency responses consistent with the types of activities and duties their employers expect them to perform during emergency response operations.

OSHA considers sound planning the first line of defense in all types of emergencies. In this guidance document, OSHA provides practical information to assist employers of security personnel in addressing employee protection and training as part of emergency planning for hazardous substance, natural disaster, and WMD-type incidents. While terrorist incidents are not emergencies that OSHA expects an employer to reasonably anticipate, by tailoring emergency plans to reflect the reasonably predictable "worst-case" scenario under which security personnel might work, employers may use these plans to guide decisions regarding appropriate training and personal protective equipment (PPE).

This document does not include any evaluation or discussion of security guard licensing. It is important to note, however, that some states have licensing programs for security personnel, including different levels of licensing in some cases. The licensing process in these states often includes classroom training and could include training directly related to the role of security personnel during emergencies. The state governments should be consulted regarding their respective licensing programs. Furthermore, this guidance document does not address the potential hazards associated with workplace violence during such emergency incidents. Compliance assistance information concerning workplace violence may be found on OSHA's Workplace Violence Safety and Health Topics webpage at www.osha.gov.

Edwin G. Foulke, Jr.
Assistant Secretary of Labor
Occupational Safety and Health

This document is not a standard or regulation, and it creates no new legal obligations. This document is advisory in nature, informational in content, and is intended to assist employers in providing a safe and healthful workplace. Pursuant to the *Occupational Safety and Health Act,* employers must comply with hazard-specific safety and health standards promulgated by OSHA or by a state with an OSHA-approved state plan. In addition, pursuant to Section 5(a)(1), the General Duty Clause of the Act, employers must provide their employees with a workplace free from recognized hazards likely to cause death or serious physical harm. Employers can be cited for violating the General Duty Clause if there is a recognized hazard and they do not take reasonable steps to prevent or abate the hazard. However, failure to implement any recommendations in this guidance document is not, in itself, a violation of the General Duty Clause. Citations can only be based on standards, regulations, and the General Duty Clause

Hazardous Substance Releases and WMD Incidents

The release of hazardous substances can result from a number of incidents and involve a wide variety of substances and hazards. From a release of a hazardous gas, such as chlorine, from damaged piping at a water treatment plant to a spill from an overturned truck hauling hydrochloric acid, the range of possible scenarios, hazardous substances, and associated hazards is extensive. Hazardous substance releases can occur in numerous forms, such as gases, liquids, dusts, and other forms, and may result from a wide array of incidents, such as an industrial accident, natural disasters, vehicle accidents, and other sources. In addition, with the increased threat of terrorist attacks, the range of possible scenarios is expanded.

Security personnel may play an integral part in emergency response efforts because they may be the first to discover and take action upon an emergency release of hazardous substances. Those security personnel expected to take on an emergency response role must be familiar with the potential hazardous substance releases and emergency incidents to which they may be exposed. The employer must ensure that these individuals understand the hazardous substance releases that may occur in their workplaces and the risks associated with them. If they play a key role in communicating the existence of an emergency release, they must be well-versed in emergency alerting and communication procedures, including who to contact according to their emergency response plan. A well-trained security staff can help to ensure the proper evacuation of employees and the public, the quick response of an emergency response team, and the proper handling of bystanders and representatives of the media.

In the case of chemical plants and similar facilities where chemicals are stored or handled routinely, hazardous substance releases are considered a potential threat and employers are required to develop emergency response plans to address them. Unless an employer plans to evacuate all personnel at the time of an uncontrolled release, it must have an emergency response plan

to respond to potential releases of hazardous substances and that plan helps to ensure that the employer has properly trained and prepared employees to effectively perform their duties during response operations. Using the example discussed above of a chlorine gas release resulting from damaged piping at a water treatment plant, the following scenario illustrates the role security personnel are likely to fill during such an incident.

During his normal rounds of a facility, one of the plant's security personnel, trained to the first responder awareness level, notices a chemical leak from a section of piping. The security guard immediately leaves the area and activates the alarm to notify the plant's emergency response team of the emergency. Once in a remote area away from the release, the security guard contacts the emergency response team leader and relays the information he knows about the location of the release and other pertinent details. The emergency response team leader assigns the security guard the task of controlling access to the release area from a safe remote location. The security guard performs his duties from the remote location until the response operations are completed by the emergency response team.

Whether a chemical plant or a government facility, terrorist attacks are not emergency incidents that can be reasonably anticipated by employers. While an employer may not have planned for a WMD attack, the HAZWOPER training requirements apply and the use of proper PPE is expected for any security personnel likely to have a role in response operations to any resulting hazardous substance releases. The following scenario illustrates the probable role of security personnel during a terrorist attack.

A contracted security guard working for a private bus company identifies an unmarked box at one of the company's bus stations. As the security guard approaches the box for better identification, she notices wet-like stains around the lower part of the box and a small amount of smoke or fumes coming from the box's seams. The security guard immediately backs away from the box and evacuates

all bus customers and other personnel from the station. The security guard then calls the company's designated and trained hazardous materials response team to report the box. The response team is sent to the location for response actions while simultaneously contacting local governmental emergency response authorities. The bus company also halts all bus operations in the area of the station until the emergency response team properly clears the area of the potential emergency release and declares the potential emergency over.

In both cases discussed above, security personnel serve the role of first responder awareness level and must be trained accordingly. Those employees assigned roles as first responder awareness level responders are limited to initiating emergency response procedures by notifying the proper authorities and must not attempt to stop the release or approach the release area. As discussed in the following section, "Emergency Response Roles and Training", the expected duties of security personnel are likely to be consistent with this level of training. Some employers, however, may choose to have security personnel perform duties beyond awareness level training. Ultimately, the training and PPE that security personnel must be provided must be appropriate for the roles which their employers expect them to fulfill during an emergency response to hazardous substance releases.

Emergency Response Roles and Training

OSHA's HAZWOPER standard requires that employees be trained to perform their anticipated job duties without endangering themselves or others. Specific emergency response training requirements for security personnel must be derived from the roles that they are assigned in their employer's emergency response plan. To determine the level and type of training employees need under 1910.120(q), consideration must be given to the actions an employee is expected to take in response to a release (e.g., notify authorities and evacuate, enter a danger area and stop a release), the hazards they may be exposed to while performing these actions, and the skills and knowledge they must have in order to

perform these actions safely. This determination must be based on worst-case scenarios. The following paragraphs as well as Figure 1 discuss the various roles and required training under the HAZWOPER standard.

Fiqure 1 - Emergency Response Roles and Training

What action will security personnel be expected to take during an emergency?

Initiating Emergency Response Only: Notifying authorities

First Responder Awareness Level 1910.120(q)(6)(i) Sufficient training to demonstrate competencies

Respond in a Defensive Fashion: Protect nearby persons, property or the environment from a safe distance

First Responder Operations Level 1910.120(q)(6)(ii) 8 hours of training or sufficient experience to demonstrate competencies

Respond in an Aggressive Fashion: These individuals approach the point of release to stop the hazardous substance release

Hazardous Materials (HAZMAT) Technician or Specialist 1910.120(q)(6)(iii) or (q)(6)(iv) 24 hours of training and specified competencies

Assume Control of the Incident: Incident Commanders assume control of the incident scene beyond the first responder awareness level

On Scene Incident Commander 1910.120(q)(6)(v) 24 hours of trainiing equal to first responder operations level and specified competencies

Skilled Support: Providing immediate, short-term support work at the scene

Skilled Support Personnel 1910.120(q)(4) Initial briefing at emergency response site to include wearing of PPE, chemical hazards involved and duties to be performed

Specialized Support: Assist, counsel or advise the IC on specific hazardous substances at the facility

Specialist Employees 1910.120(q)(5) Sufficient training or demonstrate competency in area of specialization annually

Annual refresher training/ competency demonstration

Emergency Responders

First Responder Awareness Level – 29 CFR 1910.120(q)(6)(i)

Individuals who are likely to witness or discover a hazardous substance release and are assigned to initiate an emergency response sequence by notifying the proper authorities of the release must be trained to the first responder awareness level. Generally, the duties of security personnel will fall into this category and they should be trained accordingly, since they are likely to witness or discover a release of a hazardous substance and are expected to take no further action to control or stop the release or perform rescue in the release area.

Security personnel trained to the first responder awareness level are limited to activating an alarm, notifying appropriate authorities, and controlling access to the release from a remote area upon discovering a release requiring an emergency response. Once the site control zones and safe distances have been defined by emergency responders, security personnel trained to the awareness level may also control entry to and exit from the emergency site from a safe location. Security personnel cannot assist in setting up safe distances because they lack knowledge regarding the potential for exposure, explosions, or radiation. In other instances, security personnel at hospitals or an emergency site triage may help to maintain order and control traffic around the hospital or decontami-nation facilities. Security personnel may need to control a con-taminated individual to reduce exposures or may need to prevent contaminated victims from bypassing proper decontamination. Security personnel assigned to roles where they may come in contact with contaminated victims, their belongings, equipment, or waste would require a higher level of training (e.g., First Responder Operations Level, see below).

The standard does not specify the length of training time required, only that security personnel at the first responder awareness level (1910.120(q)(6)(i)) shall have sufficient training or have had sufficient experience to objectively demonstrate competency in the following areas:

- An understanding of what hazardous substances are, and the risks associated with them in an incident.
- An understanding of the potential outcomes associated with

an emergency created when hazardous substances are present.

- The ability to recognize the presence of hazardous substances in an emergency.
- The ability to identify hazardous substances, if possible.
- An understanding of the role of the first responder awareness level individual in the employer's emergency response plan, including site security and control, and of the *U.S. Department of Transportation's Emergency Response Guidebook*.
- The ability to realize the need for additional resources, and to make appropriate notifications to the communication center.

First Responder Operations Level – 29 CFR 1910.120(q)(6)(ii)

Security personnel who are expected to respond in a defensive manner to hazardous substance releases as part of the initial response for the purpose of protecting nearby persons, property, or the environment must be trained to the first responder operations level. Their role is to contain the release from a safe distance, to keep it from spreading, and to prevent exposures – they do not attempt to stop the release. Their defensive actions must be performed from a safe distance and may include activities such as placing absorbents, constructing dikes, or securing an area to prevent the dispersal of contaminants or agents. Operations level-trained security personnel must not enter the danger area, take any aggressive action to stop the release of hazardous substances, or perform rescue work in the release area. Those expected to take aggressive action or approach the danger area must be trained to at least the hazardous materials (HAZMAT) technician level (see below).

Security personnel at the first responder operations level (1910.120(q)(6)(ii)) must receive at least eight (8) hours of training or have had sufficient experience to objectively demonstrate competency in the following areas in addition to those listed for the awareness level:

- An understanding of the basic hazard and risk assessment techniques.
- An understanding of how to select and use proper PPE

provided to the
first responder
operational level.

- An understanding
  of basic hazardous
  materials terms.
- An understanding
  of how to perform
  basic control,
  containment
  and/or confine-

Figure 2 – PPE Training

ment operations within the capabilities of the resources and
personal protective equipment available within their unit.

- An understanding of how to implement basic decontamination procedures.
- An understanding of the relevant standard operating
  procedures and termination procedures.

Security Personnel at Higher Responder Levels

While it is not expected or common, security personnel who are
expected to respond in a fashion beyond defensive action – as
discussed under first responder operations level – must be
trained to the hazardous materials (HAZMAT) technician,
HAZMAT specialist level, or On Scene Incident Commander level,
as appropriate.

Hazardous Materials (HAZMAT) Technician Level –
29 CFR 1910.120(q)(6)(iii)

Those security personnel who will respond to releases in an
aggressive fashion for the purpose of stopping the release must
be trained to the hazardous materials (HAZMAT) technician level.
These individuals approach the point of release to plug, patch, or
otherwise stop the hazardous substance release. Security personnel
at the HAZMAT technician level must receive at least 24 hours of
training equal to the first responder operations level and, in
addition, have competency in the following areas:

- An understanding of how to implement the employer's
  emergency response plan.

- An understanding of the classification, identification and verification of known and unknown materials by using field survey instruments and equipment.
- The ability to function within an assigned role in the Incident Command System.
- An understanding of how to select and use proper specialized chemical personal protective equipment provided to the hazardous materials technician.
- An understanding of hazard and risk assessment techniques.
- The ability to perform advance control, containment, and/or confinement operations within the capabilities of the resources and personal protective equipment available within the unit.
- An understanding of and ability to implement decontamination procedures.
- An understanding of termination procedures.
- An understanding of basic chemical and toxicological terminology and behavior.

Hazardous Materials (HAZMAT) Specialist Level – 29 CFR 1910.120(q)(6)(iv)

Security personnel whose assigned duties parallel those of the hazardous materials (HAZMAT) technician and who respond to releases to provide support to HAZMAT technicians in the form of specialized knowledge of substances involved in the release are hazardous materials specialists. Their training must be consistent with 1910.120(q)(6)(iv). Security personnel at the HAZMAT specialist level must receive at least 24 hours of training equal to the technician level and, in addition, have competency in the following areas:

- An understanding of how to implement the local emergency response plan.
- An understanding of the classification, identification and verification of known and unknown materials by using advanced survey instruments and equipment.
- An understanding of the state emergency response plan.
- The ability to select and use proper specialized chemical personal protective equipment provided to the hazardous

materials specialist.

- An understanding of in-depth hazard and risk techniques.
- The ability to perform specialized control, containment, and/or confinement operations within the capabilities of the resources and personal protective equipment available.
- The ability to determine and implement decontamination procedures.
- The ability to develop a site safety and control plan.
- An understanding of chemical, radiological and toxicological terminology and behavior.

On Scene Incident Commander – 29 CFR 1910.120(q)(6)(v)

If security personnel are assigned duties by their employers consistent with the role of the On Scene Incident Commander, they must receive at least 24 hours of training equal to the first responder operations level and have competencies consistent with 1910.120(q)(6)(v). The competencies include the following:

- An understanding of and the ability to implement the employer's incident command system.
- The ability to implement the employer's emergency response plan.
- Knowledge and understanding of the hazards and risks associated with employees working in chemical protective clothing.
- The ability to implement the local emergency response plan.
- An understanding of the state emergency response plan and of the Federal Regional Response Team.
- Knowledge and understanding of the importance of decontamination procedures.

Refresher Training – 29 CFR 1910.120(q)(8)

All security personnel who are required to receive initial training as required by (q)(6) must also receive annual refresher training to maintain their skills and competencies, or demonstrate competency at least annually. The employer must assure that training is of sufficient content and duration to maintain the security personnel's

competencies for their expected duties. Refresher training may be given in segments throughout the year so long as the required refresher training has been completed by the employee's training anniversary date. Time spent by security personnel critiquing or reviewing incidents may also be credited toward their annual refresher training requirements.

Figure 3 – Annual Training

OSHA's intent is that employees complete their refresher training within twelve months of their initial training. If an employee has gone without refresher training for more than twelve months, there should be a record in the employee's file indicating why the training has been delayed and when the training will be completed. The employer must also evaluate whether the initial comprehensive training may need to be repeated. The need to repeat initial training must be determined based on the employee's familiarity with safety and health procedures and potential hazards, and must be judged on a case-by-case basis. Individual retention of information must be considered as well as the applicability of past training to the duties security personnel are assigned. Employees would not need to be retrained in those training elements for which they can demonstrate competency.

Skilled Support Personnel – 29 CFR 1910.120(q)(4)

Skilled support personnel (SSP) are those employees who are needed temporarily to perform immediate emergency support work. This category of employee was included in paragraph (q) to recognize the need at times for fast-response assistance by individuals who possess needed skills in the operation of certain equipment (e.g., earthmoving or digging equipment) in an emergency. In the case of security personnel, they may assist the Incident Commander (IC) of the response effort by providing access to secured areas or sections of a building, or by providing knowledge regarding a building's air handling facilities.

Since security personnel who may serve as SSP do not expect to regularly help in emergency response incidents and may have only minimal training, attention must be given to their proper safety and health protection at the scene before they participate in the incident. This must be accomplished by an on-site briefing that includes a discussion of the chemical and physical hazards present, the personal protective equipment (PPE) to be used, how the PPE is used and its limitations, the exact task(s) they are expected to perform, and the facility's or site's safety and health precautions and procedures.

Security personnel who are to enter contaminated areas on a regular basis can no longer be considered SSP employees, and require HAZWOPER training under paragraph (q)(6) discussed above.

Specialist Employees – 29 CFR 1910.120(q)(5)

A specialist employee is an expert who may assist, counsel, or advise the IC. Specialist employees may be individuals who work with and are trained in the hazards of a specific hazardous substance (e.g., radiological materials) and are by definition individuals specialized in their area of expertise, but do not necessarily have all of the competencies of the hazardous materials (HAZMAT) technician or HAZMAT specialist. If security personnel, in the course of their regular job duties, work with and are trained in the hazards of specific hazardous substances, they may be deemed specialist employees and provide technical assistance and advice to the IC in their area of expertise.

Specialist employees must annually receive training or demonstrate competency in the area of their specialization. Even though specialist employees are experts in their respective areas, they should also be trained in how to interact within the incident command structure (ICS), and how to follow the operating procedures established by their employer. Their training is also intended to inform them of the hazards that may be present at an emergency site.

Security personnel serving in the specialist employee role may not enter the danger area unless they are fully trained in the proper use of the required PPE and are accompanied by someone trained

to the HAZMAT technician level. Security personnel who are to enter contaminated areas on a regular basis can no longer be considered specialist employees, and they require HAZWOPER training under paragraph (q)(6) discussed above.

Personal Protective Equipment

The selection of personal protective equipment (PPE) is an important step in protecting personnel. Experienced safety and health staff should be consulted to ensure the proper selection of PPE (e.g., respirators, suits, gloves, footwear, face and eye protection) based on anticipated hazards at the emergency site. Employers must select PPE based on a hazard assessment that identifies the hazards to which security personnel are or might potentially be exposed to during an emergency incident, and ensure that selected equipment meets the requirements of 1910.120 and 1910 Subpart I. As stated previously, security personnel will typically be assigned a first responder awareness level role during emergencies and have either no or only minimal exposure to hazardous substances. This limited potential for exposure would require a lower level of PPE. Where security personnel's assigned roles include closer approach to the release area or involve potential exposures, the hazard assessment and selection of PPE must account for the higher level of potential exposures.

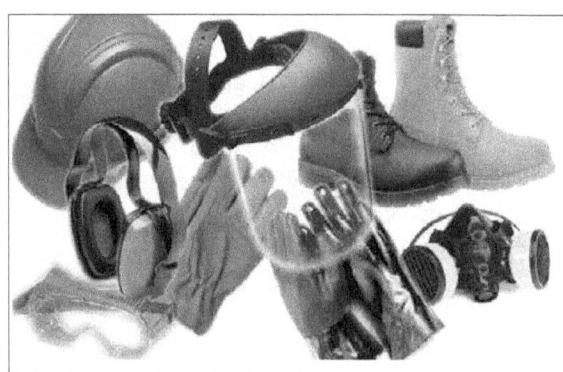

Figure 4 – Personal Protective Equipment

At facilities where the potential for hazardous substance releases can be anticipated, such as a chemical manufacturer or industrial plant utilizing hazardous substances, a hazard assessment can effectively be performed based on the hazardous substances

located on the site, potential emergency releases, and the hazards associated with them. For example, a food manufacturer may store and utilize ammonia for use in the cooling systems. The facility's safety and health staff can anticipate the potential hazardous substance releases based on site operations and perform a hazard assessment of potential exposures to site personnel, including security personnel, during an emergency release. Selection of PPE should be performed based on the hazard assessment and upgraded or downgraded throughout emergency response efforts as determined through consultation with the Incident Commander (IC) and the ICS safety officer.

The hazard assessment for PPE selection during chemical, biological, radiological, and nuclear (CBRN) incidents is a similar safety and health assessment except that many of the CBRN agents are highly toxic by both skin absorption and inhalation. Typical indicators of exposure such as odor, smoke, or fumes may not be present, and exposure monitoring is difficult for some of the compounds. Based on the hazardous substances and conditions known to be present, the site IC in charge of a response must implement appropriate emergency operations, including selection of appropriate PPE for employees who respond. To the extent feasible, employers of security personnel should consult with the IC, ICS safety officer, and/or their assigned section chief, e.g., the ICS Operations Chief, to determine appropriate PPE for their employees assisting in the response. Additionally, there may be a locally limited supply of CBRN-approved respirators and other PPE for a large response during initial emergency operations.

Respiratory Protection

When respiratory protection is an anticipated need for security or other personnel, the employer must develop and implement an effective respiratory protection program consistent with 29 CFR 1910.134(c). The written program must contain specific procedures describing how respirators will be selected, fitted, used, maintained and inspected in a particular workplace. The employer must include the following elements, as applicable, in the respiratory protection program:

- Procedures for:
  - Selecting appropriate respirators for use in the workplace.
  - Fit testing tight-fitting respirators.
  - Using respirators properly in routine situations as well as in reasonably foreseeable emergencies.
  - Cleaning, disinfecting, storing, inspecting, repairing, removing from service or discarding, and otherwise maintaining respirators. Also, you must establish schedules for these elements.
  - Ensuring adequate air supply, quantity, and flow of breathing air for atmosphere-supplying respirators.
  - Training employees in the respiratory hazards to which they are potentially exposed during routine and emergency situations.
  - Regularly evaluating the effectiveness of the program.
- Provisions for medical evaluation of employees who must use respirators.
- Training employees in the proper use of respirators (including putting them on and removing them), the limitations on their use, and their maintenance.

When selecting respirators, employers and the IC for the response must consider the chemical and physical properties of the contaminant(s), as well as the toxicity and concentration of the hazardous material and the level of oxygen present. Other selection factors are the nature and extent of the hazard, work rate, area to be covered, mobility, work requirements and conditions as well as the limitations and characteristics of the available respirators. Furthermore, respiratory protection equipment must be used within the specifications and limitations accompanying the National Institute for Occupational Safety and Health (NIOSH) certification.

When selecting appropriate respirators for security personnel, the potential contaminants as well as the expected duties of the security personnel must be considered. If security personnel are to only perform activities from a remote distance and they are not expected to have exposure to the hazards, then respirators would not be required. Those in the role of first responder awareness level, for example, would be expected to have either no or only minimal exposure. Conversely, if security personnel are to approach the release area, such as a hazardous materials

(HAZMAT) technician, then a proper respirator must be provided. As required under 1910.120(q)(3)(iv), until the IC or employer has determined the potential air contaminant(s) through air monitoring, employees engaged in the hazardous substance response and exposed to actual or potential inhalation hazards must be provided and wear a positive pressure self-contained breathing apparatus (SCBA). With respect to CBRN agents, a NIOSH CBRN agent approved respirator would be required. If the CBRN agents or their concentrations are unknown or if the exposures are expected to be high, the proper respirator would be a NIOSH CBRN agent approved SCBA. On the other hand, if CBRN agents have been quantified and the exposures are lower, a NIOSH CBRN air-purifying respirator (APR) may be appropriate, provided the oxygen levels are not deficient.

Respirators for Non-Immediately Dangerous to Life or Health (IDLH) Environments

The selection of respirators for non-IDLH environments is dependent on a number of factors. When evaluating the proper respirator, the employer must consider expected chemical concentrations, the availability of proper cartridges for contaminant(s), the proper cartridge change schedule, and the maximum use concentration for a particular cartridge. Furthermore, the employer must give consideration to the work area, the tasks to be performed, and the health and comfort of those employees donning the respirator.

A tightly constrained area may not permit the use of a SCBA even though they might be an acceptable respirator choice otherwise. Likewise, working around obstructions that can snag hoses may limit the use of airline respirators. An employee's medical condition may impact respirator selection as wearing respiratory protection poses a physical burden on the wearer. When an employee's medical condition would prohibit restrictive breathing conditions, for example, negative pressure respirators would not be an appropriate choice. Lastly, employee comfort should be a consideration during the respirator selection process. Among air-purifying respirators (APRs), powered air-purifying loose-fitting helmets have been subjectively rated the best for breathing ease, skin comfort, and in-mask temperature and humidity while filtering facepieces are rated high for lightness and

convenience. Each, however, has its own drawbacks and all these factors, as well as the respirator's assigned protection factor (APF), must be taken into account during selection. See 29 CFR 1910.134 (d)(3)(i)(A) for APF requirements provided by OSHA's Respiratory Protection standard.

When selecting respirators for non-IDLH routine use, the employer must also consider additional problems related to reasonably foreseeable emergency situations. In addition, there are substance-specific standards, such as the Asbestos, Formaldehyde, Methlyene Chloride, and Hexavalent Chromium standards, that have specific respirator selection requirements.

One of the primary considerations for APRs is whether the protection will be for gases, vapors, and/or particulates. Certain respirator and filter combinations protect against one form of contaminant, but not the others. Table 1, below, lists the three types of APRs and their characteristics.

Table 1 Air-Purifying Respirator Characteristics	
Respirator	**Characteristics**
Particulate Respirators	■ Do not protect against gases or vapors. ■ Capture particles in the air, such as dusts, mists, and fumes. ■ Generally become more effective as particles accumulate on the filter and plug spaces between the fibers. ■ Filters should be replaced when the user finds it difficult to breathe through them.
Combination Respirators	■ Normally used in atmospheres that contain hazards of both particulates and gases. ■ Have both particulate filters and gas/vapor filters. ■ May be heavier.
Gas & Vapor Respirators	■ Do not protect against airborne particles. ■ Normally used when there are only hazardous gases and vapors in the air. ■ Use chemical cartridges or canisters to remove dangerous gases or vapors. ■ Made to protect against specific gases or vapors. ■ Provide protection only as long as the cartridge's or canister's absorbing capacity is not depleted. ■ The service life of the cartridge or canister depends upon many factors and can be estimated in various ways.

Sections I. and II. of the Appendix (at pages 30 and 31) discuss respirators for different types of environments that may apply to security personnel assigned response roles at higher levels: immediately dangerous to life or health (IDLH) and CBRN environments. An employer must select the proper respiratory protection based on security personnel's expected duties, the contaminant(s) and the conditions present at the release site, the limitations of the respiratory protection available, and the respirator manufacturer specifications and guidance. The NIOSH respirator decision logic (See NIOSH Respirator Selection Logic 2004, NIOSH Publication No. 2005-100) may assist in selecting the proper respiratory protection.

Protective Clothing
General Guidelines

As mentioned earlier, emergency incidents involving hazardous substances, including CBRN agents, often include substances that are highly toxic by inhalation and/or skin absorption. While proper respiratory protection will protect security personnel from inhalation hazards, the responders can remain at risk without proper protective clothing. A key point made in the training section of this document is that security personnel are most likely to be assigned roles consistent with first responder awareness level. In this role, security personnel are not to approach the danger zone of the incident and must remain in safe areas that are free of contaminants. Accordingly, these security personnel do not face the potential for exposure to agents and, therefore, the need for protective clothing is diminished. Personnel who are designated to take on a role beyond first responder awareness level during an emergency incident must be provided protective clothing for protection against identified or potential contaminants that pose a skin hazard. Likewise, security personnel who serve as SSP or specialist employees and who may experience contaminant exposures must be provided appropriate protective clothing.

The selection of protective clothing or suits is a complex task and should be performed by knowledgeable personnel with experience in selecting protective equipment for contaminant exposure. Employers must consider the properties of the

contaminant(s), the toxicity and concentration of the hazardous material, and the tasks to be performed by those individuals wearing the clothing. Further, the performance characteristics of the clothing material against the contaminant(s) must be evaluated. The selection must consider how the material resists permeation, degradation, and penetration by contaminants involved in the incident.

The protective clothing guidance below is discussed in relation to levels of contamination, the zones of red, yellow, and green (see Figure 5). Those security personnel trained to the first responder awareness level would be expected to only take on roles in the Green Zone or further removed from the release area where there are no potential exposures. Those entering the Yellow Zone would minimally be trained to the first responder operations level and those entering the Red Zone would be trained to at least the hazardous materials (HAZMAT) technician level (see Training section, above). These zones of Red, Yellow, and Green are available to be used as complimentary guidance for personal protective equipment selection based on the level of knowledge about the emergency release. The use of the zones is neither mandatory nor exclusionary of other site control concepts, such as the traditional Exclusion (Hot), Contamination Reduction (Warm), and Support (Cold) Zones.

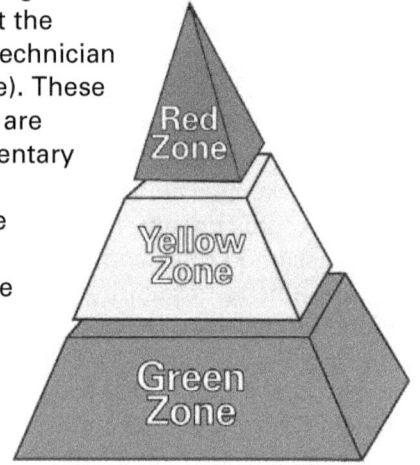

Figure 5 – OSHA's Response Zones

Red Zone areas are where significant contamination with hazardous substances or CBRN agents has been confirmed or is strongly suspected but the area has not been characterized. This area is presumed to be life-threatening from both skin contact and inhalation. Level A protection (1910.120 Appendix B)

is generally needed when the active release is still occurring, or the release has stopped but there is no information about the duration of the release or the airborne concentrations of substances. Responders going into a known release area where hazardous substances are suspected should be in a fully encapsulating protective suit until monitoring results allow for other decisions. Level A protection should be consistent with the description in 1910.120 Appendix B and, where CBRN agents are involved, suits should be appropriate for CBRN agents, e.g., meets the requirements of National Fire Protection Association (NFPA) 1994-2001, has been approved by NIOSH as a CBRN approved SCBA, has been tested by a third party such as the U.S. Army's Joint Program Executive Office for Chemical and Biological Defense (JPEO-CBD) (formerly Soldier and Biological Chemical Command (SBCCOM)) or has undergone other manufacturer testing.

In addition to the requirements specified in 1910.120(q)(3), practices prudent for the Red Zone where the level of contamination or exposure is unknown include, but are not limited to, the following:

- Don appropriate PPE. A SCBA is required where the level of exposure is unknown and until the Incident Commander can determine that a decreased level of respiratory protection is appropriate.
- Assess the emergency site. Is there a spill, leak, or fire? Can the contaminant(s) be identified from a distance, e.g., Any labeling? Who is at risk? What actions are necessary?
- Develop an incident response plan and respond appropriately. Continually reassess the situation and modify the response and zone boundaries as appropriate.
- Limit responders to those actively performing response operations.
- Implement evacuation where necessary to protect life.
- Establish and follow effective lines of communication. Communicate status with Incident Command.
- Enforce appropriate Yellow Zone and Green Zone practices.

Yellow Zone areas are where contamination with hazardous substances or CBRN agents is possible but active release has ended and initial monitoring data exists. Areas in close proximity to the release area or that are known to be contaminated and certain job activities on the periphery of the release area should be considered for this zone. Risk factors that should be considered include determining the relative risk for job activities from skin contact and absorption potential, proximity to the incident, and wind directions. Protective clothing should be selected by knowledgeable personnel based on the specific hazards and characteristics of the identified contaminants.

In addition to the requirements specified in 1910.120(q)(3), practices prudent for the Yellow Zone where the area is known to be contaminated include, but are not limited to, the following:

- Don appropriate PPE. Based on monitoring results, the Incident Commander must select PPE appropriate to the exposures and related hazards.
- Perform tasks within the characterized zone as per the incident response plan.
- Limit those in the Yellow Zone to those actively performing response-related duties.
- Establish and follow effective lines of communication. Plan for and be prepared to request assistance and/or provide emergency backup to responders performing actions in the Red Zone.
- Enforce appropriate Green Zone practices.

Green Zone areas are where contamination with hazardous substances or CBRN agents is unlikely. This zone covers the area beyond the expected significant dispersal range of the initial release and secondary contamination range caused by traffic and emergency responders. Persons in this area are not expected to be exposed to hazards presented by the incident contaminants. Generally, protective clothing will not be required for personnel in this area, including those security personnel at the first responder awareness level. Because of the concern or potential for a minimal level of transient or unknown exposures in the aftermath of an emergency incident, prudent practices for the Green Zone include, but are not limited to, the following:

- Inform people of the location of the release and the control zones.
- Provide information regarding signs and symptoms of exposure.
- Suggest a means for reporting suspected exposures.
- Suggest attention to general hygiene practices.
- Provide information on voluntary use of PPE.

Protective Clothing Guidance in the Appendix at page 34 provides references to assist in the selection of chemical- and CBRN-protective clothing where the emergency response roles of security personnel necessitate such protective equipment, i.e., those personnel assigned to take action closer to the release area such as HAZMAT technician or HAZMAT specialist level personnel.

General References

OSHA References

OSHA, "Emergency Preparedness and Response Safety and Health Topics Web Page."
www.osha.gov/SLTC/emergencypreparedness/index.html

OSHA, "Workplace Violence Safety and Health Topics Web Page."
www.osha.gov/SLTC/workplaceviolence/index.html

OSHA, "Evacuation Plans and Procedures eTool."
www.osha.gov/SLTC/etools/evacuation/index.html

Additional References

DOT ERG2004, "Emergency Response Guidebook."

FEMA 508-6, "Typed Resource Definitions, Law Enforcement and Security Resources."

FEMA 426, "Reference Manual to Mitigate Potential Terrorist Attacks Against Buildings."

FEMA 427, "Primer for Design of Commercial Buildings to Mitigate Terrorist Attacks."

FEMA 452, "Risk Assessment: A How-To Guide to Mitigate Potential Terrorist Attacks."

NIOSH 2005-149, "NIOSH Pocket Guide to Chemical Hazards."

USPS, "Best Practices for Mail Center Security."

Abbreviations

APER – Air-purifying escape respirator

APF – Assigned protection factor

APR – Air-purifying respirator

CBRN – Chemical, biological, radiological, and nuclear

HAZMAT – Hazardous materials

HAZWOPER – Hazardous Waste Operations and Emergency Response standard

IC – Incident Commander

ICS – Incident command structure

IDLH – Immediately dangerous to life or health

NFPA – National Fire Protection Association

NIOSH – National Institute for Occupational Safety and Health

PPE – Personal protective equipment

SAR – Supplied-air respirator

SCBA – Self-contained breathing apparatus

SSP – Skilled support personnel

WMD – Weapon(s) of mass destruction

Appendix

As discussed earlier in this publication, the expected duties of security personnel are commonly consistent with the first responder awareness level of training. Some employers, however, may choose to assign security personnel duties beyond awareness level training. In each case, employers must assure that the training and PPE security personnel are provided are appropriate for the roles they are expected to fulfill during an emergency response. This appendix provides a discussion of respirators and protective clothing often necessary with higher levels of emergency response duties and associated training levels.

I. Respirators for Immediately Dangerous to Life or Health (IDLH) Environments

Atmospheres that are IDLH are those where an atmospheric concentration of any toxic, corrosive or asphyxiant substance poses an immediate threat to life or would cause irreversible or delayed adverse health effects or would interfere with an individual's ability to escape from a dangerous atmosphere. Oxygen-deficient atmospheres and those atmospheres that are not or cannot be estimated must be treated as IDLH environments.

OSHA's Respiratory Protection standard, 1910.134, requires that employers provide atmosphere-supplying respirators for employees who are to enter IDLH atmospheres. Atmosphere-supplying respirators are designed to provide breathable air from a clean air source other than the surrounding contaminated work atmosphere. They include SCBA units, combination respirators, and supplied-air respirators (SARs). Specifically, 1910.134(d)(2) requires either a full

Figure 6 – Air Purifying Respirator (APR)

facepiece pressure demand SCBA with a minimum 30-minutes service life or a combination full facepiece pressure demand SAR with an auxillary self-contained air supply.

Air-purifying respirators (APRs) are not permitted to be used in IDLH and oxygen-deficient atmospheres. An APR works by filtering or scrubbing harmful substances from the air as the user breathes in the surrounding air through respirator filters or cartridges that contain sorbents. An APR can range from a simple, disposable mask to sophisticated devices. Unlike SCBAs and combination SARs with a self-contained air supply, APRs do not supply the needed oxygen to the wearer.

In addition, 1910.134(g)(3) requires that prior to entering an IDLH environment, standby employees located outside the IDLH atmosphere must be available to provide an effective emergency rescue. Standby employees must be equipped with the appropriate equipment such as pressure-demand or other positive pressure self-contained breathing apparatus (SCBA), or a pressure-demand or other positive pressure supplied-air respirator with auxiliary SCBA. The outside personnel maintain communication with the entrant(s) and may perform outside rescue and other duties that do not interfere with their primary role of support, but are required to be trained and suitably equipped to enter the IDLH, if necessary to provide emergency rescue.

II. Respirators for CBRN Agent Environments

For security personnel who will respond to emergency incidents involving potential exposure to CBRN agents, the employer must select and provide respirators that are CBRN agent approved by NIOSH. Currently, NIOSH has only certified a number of SCBA, APR, and air-purifying escape respirator (APER) units.

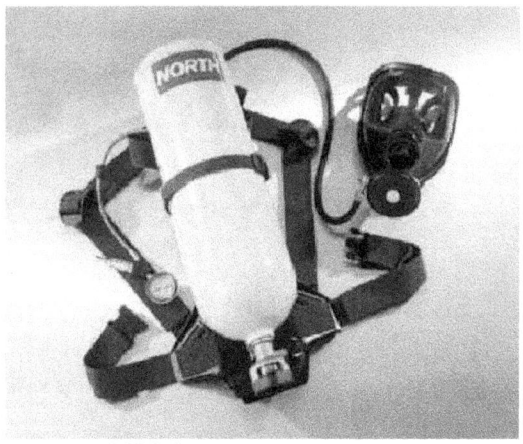

Figure 7 – SCBA Gear

31

CBRN-Approved SCBAs

In response to a CBRN incident, security personnel must use NIOSH-approved CBRN SCBA respirators when the types of inhalation hazards and their concentrations are unknown or are expected to be high. CRBN SCBA respirators must also be chosen when the atmospheres are known IDLH or oxygen-deficient. NIOSH approval under the program signifies that an SCBA is expected to provide needed protection to first responders in situations where an act of terror has released harmful chemical, biological, or radioactive materials into the air. SCBAs approved by NIOSH for CBRN hazards are available on the NIOSH website.

To determine if a given SCBA has been tested and certified by NIOSH for use by emergency responders in CBRN environments:

- Look to see if the CBRN Agent Approval label is on the respirator. If an SCBA is CBRN-approved by NIOSH, it will always carry a NIOSH CBRN Agent Approval label (See Figure 8). If this label is not on the SCBA, the device is not approved by NIOSH for use by emergency responders in CBRN environments.

- Additional information is provided through the NIOSH matrix-style approval labels found in the "Instruction Manual" for the respirator. The "Instruction Manual" is shipped by the manufacturer with the respirator.

National Institute for
Occupational Safety and Health

NIOSH

CBRN Agent Approved

See Instructions for Required Component Part Numbers, Accessories, and Additional Cautions and Limitations of Use

Figure 8 – NIOSH CBRN Agent Approval Label

Once chosen, care must be given to the proper use of the SCBA consistent with the respirator instruction manual. Furthermore, direct contact with CBRN agents requires proper handling of the SCBA after each use and between multiple entries during the same use. Decontamination and disposal procedures must be followed. If contaminated with liquid, chemical disposal of the SCBA after decontamination is necessary. Based on evaluation of the respirator contamination and condition, disposal of the SCBA may also be necessary for SCBAs contaminated with biological or radiological agents.

CBRN-Approved APRs and APERs
A CBRN APR full facepiece respirator provides a lower level of protection than a SCBA and should generally only be selected for security personnel once conditions are understood and exposures are determined to be at lower levels. A CBRN APR respirator must not be used in atmospheres where hazard concentrations are IDLH or oxygen-deficient, or where the concentrations are not fully characterized. If unknown or high levels of hazard are encountered due to a secondary hazard source during normal use, the user should immediately leave the area. NIOSH is currently drafting detailed user guidance for the CBRN APR.

NIOSH has also approved some air-purifying escape respirators (APERs) for escape from CBRN environments. A NIOSH approval signifies the APER is expected to protect the general working population in escape scenarios from CBRN exposures at a terrorist incident. The approved APERs use a chemical cartridge combined with a particulate filter to purify contaminated air and are approved for 15- and 30-minute escapes. Selection of these CBRN APERs for security personnel must be limited to those individuals whose expected duties do not require them to enter or approach the danger area of a CBRN release. Security personnel trained to and expected to perform duties consistent with the first responder operations level or higher must not be provided an APER for their response to a CBRN incident. APERs are certified solely for escape from CBRN environments. Conversely, those security personnel trained to and expected to perform duties of the first responder awareness level may be provided CBRN APERs for escape from a CBRN release area. The roles of these individuals during an emergency release call for the initiation of a response effort by notifying authorities and additional actions from the safety of a

remote area away from the danger of the release.

Three types of labels are included with CBRN APR and APER respirators: a full canister label located on the canister, a matrix-style canister approval label, and a matrix-style respirator approval label. The matrix-style approval labels are part of the user's instructions or are included as an insert with the packaging. All three labels include a NIOSH Approval number and CBRN protection level in addition to other respirator/canister information. APRs and APERs approved by NIOSH for CBRN hazards are available on the NIOSH website (www.cdc.gov/niosh).

III. Protective Clothing Guidance

The selection of chemical- or CBRN-protective clothing is a complex task that should be performed by experienced and knowledgeable personnel. These personnel should have experience in selecting protective equipment for the particular agent and possess knowledge of available clothing materials. Clothing for security personnel should be selected by evaluating the performance characteristics of the material against the particular contaminants and the site- and task-specific conditions and requirements. The following references provide guidance on selecting chemical- and CBRN-protective clothing.

- Guide for the Selection of Personal Protection Equipment for Emergency First Responders. National Institute of Justice (NIJ). Guide 102–00. November 2002. www.ojp.usdoj.gov/nij/pubs-sum/191518.htm.
- Guide for the Selection of Chemical and Biological Decontamination Equipment for Emergency First Responders. National Institute of Justice (NIJ). Guide 103-00. October 2001. www.ojp.usdoj.gov/nij/pubs-sum/189724.htm.
- Recommendations for Chemical Protective Clothing - A Companion to the NIOSH Pocket Guide to Chemical Hazards. National Institute for Occupational Safety and Health (NIOSH). NTIS No. PB98-137730. February 1998. www.cdc.gov/niosh/ncpc/ncpc1.html.
- A Guide for Evaluating the Performance of Chemical Protective Clothing. National Institute for Occupational Safety and Health (NIOSH). DHHS (NIOSH) Publication No. 90-109. June 1990. www.cdc.gov/niosh/90-109.html.
- Standard on Vapor-Protective Ensembles for Hazardous

Materials Emergencies. National Fire Protection Association (NFPA). NFPA 1991. 2005 edition. www.nfpa.org.

- Standard on Liquid Splash-Protective Ensembles and Clothing for Hazardous Materials Emergencies. National Fire Protection Association (NFPA). NFPA 1992. 2005 edition. www.nfpa.org.
- Standard on Protective Ensembles for Chemical/Biological Terrorism Incidents. National Fire Protection Association (NFPA). NFPA 1994. 2001 edition. www.nfpa.org.
- Emergency Response Guidebook. ERG2004. Department of Transportation, The Office of Hazardous Materials Safety. 2004. http://hazmat.dot.gov/pubs/erg/gydebook.htm.

OSHA Assistance

OSHA can provide extensive help through a variety of programs, including technical assistance about effective safety and health programs, state plans, workplace consultations, voluntary protection programs, strategic partnerships, training and education, and more. An overall commitment to workplace safety and health can add value to your business, to your workplace, and to your life.

Safety and Health Program Management Guidelines

Effective management of employee safety and health protection is a decisive factor in reducing the extent and severity of work-related injuries and illnesses and their related costs. In fact, an effective safety and health program forms the basis of good employee protection and can save time and money (about $4 for every dollar spent) and increase productivity and reduce employee injuries, illnesses, and related workers' compensation costs.

To assist employers and employees in developing effective safety and health programs, OSHA published recommended Safety and Health Program Management Guidelines (54 Federal Register (16): 3904-3916, January 26, 1989). These voluntary guidelines can be applied to all places of employment covered by OSHA.

The guidelines identify four general elements critical to the development of a successful safety and health management system:

- Management leadership and employee involvement,
- Worksite analysis,
- Hazard prevention and control, and
- Safety and health training.

The guidelines recommend specific actions, under each of these general elements, to achieve an effective safety and health program. The *Federal Register* notice is available online at www.osha.gov.

State Programs

The *Occupational Safety and Health Act of 1970* (OSH Act) encourages states to develop and operate their own job safety and health plans. OSHA approves and monitors these plans. Twenty-four states, Puerto Rico and the Virgin Islands currently operate approved state plans: 22 cover both private and public (state and local government) employment; Connecticut, New Jersey, New York and the Virgin Islands cover the public sector only. States and territories with their own OSHA-approved occupational safety and health plans must adopt standards identical to, or at least as effective as, the Federal OSHA standards.

Consultation Services

Consultation assistance is available on request to employers who want help in establishing and maintaining a safe and healthful workplace. Largely funded by OSHA, the service is provided at no cost to the employer. Primarily developed for smaller employers with more hazardous operations, the consultation service is delivered by state governments employing professional safety and health consultants. Comprehensive assistance includes an appraisal of all mechanical systems, work practices, and occupational safety and health hazards of the workplace and all aspects of the employer's present job safety and health program. In addition, the service offers assistance to employers in developing and implementing an effective safety and health program. No penalties are proposed or citations issued for hazards identified by the consultant. OSHA provides consultation assistance to the employer with the assurance that his or her name and firm and any information about the workplace will not be routinely reported to OSHA enforcement staff.

Under the consultation program, certain exemplary employers may request participation in OSHA's Safety and Health Achievement Recognition Program (SHARP). Eligibility for participation in SHARP includes receiving a comprehensive consultation visit, demonstrating exemplary achievements in workplace safety and health by abating all identified hazards, and developing an excellent safety and health program.

Employers accepted into SHARP may receive an exemption from programmed inspections (not complaint or accident investiga-

tion inspections) for a period of 1 year. For more information concerning consultation assistance, see OSHA's website at www.osha.gov.

Voluntary Protection Programs (VPP)

Voluntary Protection Programs and on-site consultation services, when coupled with an effective enforcement program, expand employee protection to help meet the goals of the OSH Act. The VPPs motivate others to achieve excellent safety and health results in the same outstanding way as they establish a cooperative relationship between employers, employees, and OSHA.

For additional information on VPP and how to apply, contact the OSHA regional offices listed at the end of this publication.

Strategic Partnership Program

OSHA's Strategic Partnership Program, the newest member of OSHA's cooperative programs, helps encourage, assist, and recognize the efforts of partners to eliminate serious workplace hazards and achieve a high level of employee safety and health. Whereas OSHA's Consultation Program and VPP entail one-on-one relationships between OSHA and individual worksites, most strategic partnerships seek to have a broader impact by building cooperative relationships with groups of employers and employees. These partnerships are voluntary, cooperative relationships between OSHA, employers, employee representatives, and others (e.g., trade unions, trade and professional associations, universities, and other government agencies).

For more information on this and other cooperative programs, contact your nearest OSHA office, or visit OSHA's website at www.osha.gov.

Alliance Program

Through the Alliance Program, OSHA works with groups committed to safety and health, including businesses, trade or professional organizations, unions and educational institutions, to leverage resources and expertise to develop compliance assistance tools and resources and share information with employers and employees to help prevent injuries, illnesses and fatalities in the workplace.

Alliance Program agreements have been established with a wide variety of industries including meat, apparel, poultry, steel, plastics, maritime, printing, chemical, construction, paper and telecommunications. These agreements are addressing many safety and health hazards and at-risk audiences, including silica, fall protection, amputations, immigrant workers, youth and small businesses. By meeting the goals of the Alliance Program agreements (training and education, outreach and communication, and promoting the national dialogue on workplace safety and health), OSHA and the Alliance Program participants are developing and disseminating compliance assistance information and resources for employers and employees such as electronic assistance tools, fact sheets, toolbox talks, and training programs.

OSHA Training and Education

OSHA area offices offer a variety of information services, such as compliance assistance, technical advice, publications, audiovisual aids and speakers for special engagements. OSHA's Training Institute in Arlington Heights, IL, provides basic and advanced courses in safety and health for federal and state compliance officers, state consultants, federal agency personnel, and private sector employers, employees, and their representatives.

The OSHA Training Institute also has established OSHA Training Institute Education Centers to address the increased demand for its courses from the private sector and from other federal agencies. These centers include colleges, universities, and nonprofit training organizations that have been selected after a competition for participation in the program.

OSHA also provides funds to nonprofit organizations, through grants, to conduct workplace training and education in subjects where OSHA believes there is a lack of workplace training. Grants are awarded annually. Grant recipients are expected to contribute 20 percent of the total grant cost.

For more information on grants, training, and education, contact the OSHA Training Institute, Office of Training and Education, 2020 South Arlington Heights Road, Arlington Heights, IL 60005, (847) 297-4810, or see *Outreach* on OSHA's website at www.osha.gov. For further information on any OSHA program, contact your nearest OSHA regional office listed at the end of this publication.

Information Available Electronically

OSHA has a variety of materials and tools available on its website at www.osha.gov. These include electronic compliance assistance tools, such as Safety and Health Topics, eTools, Expert Advisors; regulations, directives and publications; videos and other information for employers and employees. OSHA's software programs and compliance assistance tools walk you through challenging safety and health issues and common problems to find the best solutions for your workplace.

A wide variety of OSHA materials, including standards, interpretations, directives and more can be purchased on CD-ROM from the U.S. Government Printing Office, Superintendent of Documents, toll-free phone (866) 512-1800.

OSHA Publications

OSHA has an extensive publications program. For a listing of free or sales items, visit OSHA's website at www.osha.gov or contact the OSHA Publications Office, U.S. Department of Labor, 200 Constitution Avenue, NW, N-3101, Washington, DC 20210: Telephone (202) 693-1888 or fax to (202) 693-2498.

Contacting OSHA

To report an emergency, file a complaint, or seek OSHA advice, assistance, or products, call (800) 321-OSHA or contact your nearest OSHA Regional or Area office listed at the end of this publication. The teletypewriter (TTY) number is (877) 889-5627.

Written correspondence can be mailed to the nearest OSHA Regional or Area Office listed at the end of this publication or to OSHA's national office at: U.S. Department of Labor, Occupational Safety and Health Administration, 200 Constitution Avenue, N.W., Washington, DC 20210.

By visiting OSHA's website at www.osha.gov, you can also:

- file a complaint online,

- submit general inquiries about workplace safety and health electronically, and

- find more information about OSHA and occupational safety and health.

OSHA Regional Offices

Region I
(CT,* ME, MA, NH, RI, VT*)
JFK Federal Building, Room E340
Boston, MA 02203
(617) 565-9860

Region II
(NJ,* NY,* PR,* VI*)
201 Varick Street, Room 670
New York, NY 10014
(212) 337-2378

Region III
(DE, DC, MD,* PA, VA,* WV)
The Curtis Center
170 S. Independence Mall West
Suite 740 West
Philadelphia, PA 19106-3309
(215) 861-4900

Region IV
(AL, FL, GA, KY,* MS, NC,* SC,* TN*)
61 Forsyth Street, SW, Room 6T50
Atlanta, GA 30303
(404) 562-2300

Region V
(IL, IN,* MI,* MN,* OH, WI)
230 South Dearborn Street
Room 3244
Chicago, IL 60604
(312) 353-2220

Region VI
(AR, LA, NM,* OK, TX)
525 Griffin Street, Room 602
Dallas, TX 75202
(972) 850-4145

Region VII
(IA,* KS, MO, NE)
Two Pershing Square
2300 Main Street, Suite 1010
Kansas City, MO 64108
(816) 283-8745

Region VIII
(CO, MT, ND, SD, UT,* WY*)
1999 Broadway, Suite 1690
PO Box 46550
Denver, CO 80202-5716
(720) 264-6550

Region IX
(American Samoa, AZ,* CA,* Guam,
HI,* NV,* Northern Mariana Islands)
90 7th Street, Suite 18-100
San Francisco, CA 94103
(415) 625-2547

Region X
(AK,* ID, OR,* WA*)
1111 Third Avenue, Suite 715
Seattle, WA 98101-3212
(206) 553-5930

* These states and territories operate their own OSHA-approved job safety and health programs (Connecticut, New Jersey, New York and the Virgin Islands plans cover public employees only). States with approved programs must adopt standards identical to, or at least as effective as, the Federal OSHA standards.

Note: To get contact information for OSHA Area Offices, OSHA-approved State Plans and OSHA Consultation Projects, please visit us online at www.osha.gov or call us at 1-800-321-OSHA.

www.ingramcontent.com/pod-product-compliance
Lightning Source LLC
Chambersburg PA
CBHW051824170526
45167CB00005B/2151